SPOTLIGHT ON
IMMIGRATION AND MIGRATION

THE GROWTH OF THE AMERICAN CITY

IMMIGRANTS AND MIGRANTS TRAVEL FOR WORK

Mina Flores

PowerKiDS press

NEW YORK

Published in 2016 by The Rosen Publishing Group, Inc.
29 East 21st Street, New York, NY 10010

Editor: Sarah Machajewski
Book Design: Samantha DeMartin

Photo Credits: Cover Fototeca Storica Nazionale./Hulton Archive/Getty Images; pp. 5, 8–9, 9 (inset), 11 (both), 13, 14–15, 15 (inset), 22 courtesy of Library of Congress; p. 7 Museum of the City of New York/ Byron Collection/Archive Photos/Getty Images; p. 17 Kean Collection/Archive Photos/Getty Images; p. 19 Archive Photos/Archive Photos/Getty Images; p. 21 (inset) Welgos/Archive Photos/Getty Images; p. 21 (main) Jack Aiello/Shutterstock.com.

Cataloging-in-Publication Data

Flores, Mina.
The growth of the American city : immigrants and migrants travel for work / by Mina Flores.
p. cm. — (Spotlight on immigration and migration)
Includes index.
ISBN 978-1-5081-4076-4 (pbk.)
ISBN 978-1-5081-4077-1 (6-pack)
ISBN 978-1-5081-4079-5 (library binding)
1. Cities and towns — America — Juvenile literature. I. Title.
HT152.F56 2016
307.76—d23

Manufactured in the United States of America

CPSIA Compliance Information: Batch #BW16PK: For further information contact Rosen Publishing, New York, New York at 1-800-237-9932.

CONTENTS

CHANGE COMES TO AMERICA

The Industrial Revolution was a time when manufacturing processes changed from producing goods by hand to producing goods by machine. It started in Great Britain around 1760 and reached America a few **decades** later. Over the next century, America's economy changed from one based on farming and agriculture to one based on manufacturing.

People looking for work started to **migrate** to cities from rural parts of the United States. Factories were being built in the cities, and there was a huge need for factory workers. In 1790, the five most populated cities in the United States were Boston, New York, Philadelphia, Baltimore, and Charleston. With a population of about 33,000, New York City was the largest. Many historians feel the Industrial Revolution changed people's way of life more than any other event in American history.

Many **immigrants** contributed to the progress of the Industrial Revolution. In fact, one of the first signs of **industrialization** in the United States was Samuel Slater's first water-powered **textile** mill in Rhode Island. Slater was a British immigrant.

MAJOR POPULATION GROWTH

Though signs of industrialization appeared in the late 1700s, the Industrial Revolution really took hold in the United States in the late 1800s. By 1900, three American cities had a population of more than 1 million. New York City had about 3.5 million people, Chicago had nearly 1.7 million people, and Philadelphia's population was around 1.3 million.

This great population growth happened because people already living in the United States moved to cities to be close to the factories where they worked. Also, immigrants arriving in the United States looked for work in cities rather than in rural communities. At first, people moved so quickly and in such large numbers that cities and towns weren't ready for them. People built shantytowns on the edges of cities when no other housing was available.

Shantytowns are areas where the homes are mostly wooden shacks. Shantytowns often sprang up on the outer edges of towns and cities.

LIFE IN AMERICA'S CITIES

Industrialization brought great changes to the United States, such as the creation of many jobs and the growth of cities. However, there were bad changes along with the good. One of the biggest problems was the creation of poor living conditions for people in cities. Many places hadn't yet developed **sewer systems**. Garbage and human waste ran in the streets' gutters. This attracted rats and bugs, which spread sicknesses.

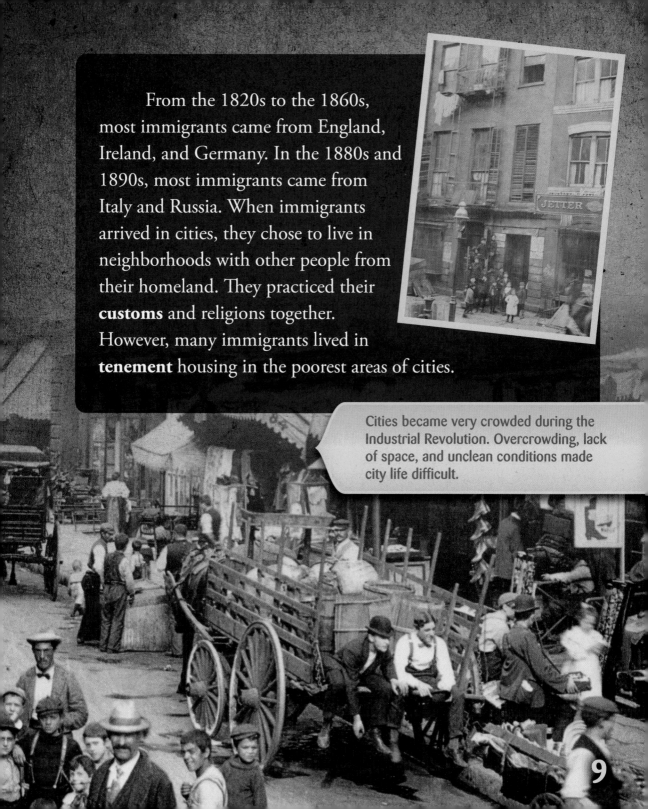

From the 1820s to the 1860s, most immigrants came from England, Ireland, and Germany. In the 1880s and 1890s, most immigrants came from Italy and Russia. When immigrants arrived in cities, they chose to live in neighborhoods with other people from their homeland. They practiced their **customs** and religions together. However, many immigrants lived in **tenement** housing in the poorest areas of cities.

Cities became very crowded during the Industrial Revolution. Overcrowding, lack of space, and unclean conditions made city life difficult.

THE REALITY OF WORKING CONDITIONS

Many immigrants came to the United States with nothing. They had little money, few belongings, and nowhere to live. The first step for many was to find work. Most immigrants took jobs in factories and coal mines.

Working conditions in these places were very poor. Wages were low, and workdays were long. Air in the factories often contained harmful chemicals that were used to manufacture goods. It wasn't uncommon for workers to pass out from exhaustion. Some workers' toes froze off because factories were rarely heated during winter.

During the 1830s and 1840s, factory workers labored 12 to 14 hours each day, 6 days a week. Safety standards didn't exist at this time, and sometimes fires broke out. Conditions in coal mines were just as hard, unsafe, and deadly as they were in factories.

These images show factory workers and coal miners around the turn of the 20th century. These jobs were very difficult.

PUTTING KIDS TO WORK

Although it may be hard to imagine today, children were often sent to work in factories. The use of child labor was common in industrial America. Factory owners liked to hire children. They could pay children less than adults. Also, a child's hands were small enough to reach into the tight spaces of the machines. This was helpful when it came to tasks such as changing spools of thread in textile mills.

Children worked in factories because they needed to help support their family. However, it came at a cost. Children commonly worked 12- or 14-hour days for as little as a dollar a week. They faced the same poor conditions as adult workers. They were often beaten and overworked. Since they were working, they couldn't go to school.

Many immigrant children and their parents worked in factories. Immigrant workers usually worked for less pay than American workers and usually didn't protest the poor working conditions. They were often considered stupid when they couldn't understand the English spoken by their bosses.

Many social **reformers** worked to end child labor practices. In 1938, the Fair Labor Standards Act was passed, which created a minimum age of employment and limited the hours young people could work. Adult immigrants and women replaced the children who could no longer work.

UNIONIZING FOR CHANGE

Part of the reason bad working conditions existed is because they benefited factory owners and industrialists. They profited from overworking and underpaying immigrant workers in their factories and mines. Many people didn't feel comfortable speaking out because they feared losing their job.

Another labor **union** was the Industrial Workers of the World (IWW). It was also called the Wobblies. This organization formed in 1905.

However, people soon began to **rebel** against the terrible conditions. During the 1800s, workers started labor unions to fight for their rights. The main issues were safety, working conditions, wages, and the length of the workday. One of the first unions was the Knights of Labor. It was started in 1869 by nine tailors in Philadelphia.

Samuel Gompers was an British Jewish immigrant who came to America from London. In 1886, he organized a group called the American Federation of Labor (AFL). It was a national organization of trade unions. This group used strikes to get better contracts and conditions for workers.

SAMUEL GOMPERS

I.W.W.
WE WANT 12 HOURS A DAY WORK
SATURDAY 16 HOURS
UR BOSSES THINK I

AMERICA TURNS ANTIUNION

The efforts of social reformers and unions did much to change working conditions in factories. Many laws were passed in the early 1900s that improved conditions for workers. For example, the average workday was reduced to eight hours. Despite such successes, many unions that formed during this period either failed or didn't become strong enough until later in the 20th century. Unions weren't popular because strikes and occasional conflict unsettled city life.

In 1875, a group called the Working Men's Benevolent Association (WBA) organized a strike for workers to walk out of the coal mines. The strike was broken, and the WBA lost power. A group called the Molly Maguires became more powerful, but their activism efforts often turned violent. The accusations of violence and the arrests against the Mollies, as they were called, turned many people against unions.

The Molly Maguires started in Ireland. Historians believe Irish immigrants brought this group to the United States in the 1800s. The organization had a big presence among Irish Americans who lived near and worked in the coal mines of Pennsylvania.

CONNECTING AMERICA BY RAIL

The quick growth of America's cities was mostly due to the huge number of immigrants who came to a new country and joined its workforce. The movement of immigrants to cities and of people migrating from the country was aided by the development of the railroad.

Building the railroad required large labor forces. When jobs became available, many immigrant groups were there to answer the call. One immigrant group in particular, the Chinese, was very important in building the Central Pacific Railroad. Other immigrant groups, such as the Irish, were important in building railroads, too.

In 1865, there were about 35,000 miles (56,300 km) of track in the United States. By 1900, that number had grown to about 215,000 miles (346,000 km). The building of railroads was necessary for industry in America to grow. It allowed the goods manufactured in the factories to be carried into and out of cities and towns.

The railroad was one of the most important developments of the Industrial Revolution. It opened up the American West, led to the growth of towns and cities, and created many new economic opportunities.

19

CHANGING WAYS OF LIFE

The growth of America's industries also caused cities to develop a **reputation** based on the goods that were created there. For example, Houston, Texas, was known for producing railroad cars. Birmingham, Alabama, was known for its steel. Glass was made in Toledo, Ohio. New **technologies** helped change the way cities looked, too. The development of iron and steel allowed cities to build taller buildings, since these **materials** could support more weight.

The invention of passenger elevators in 1857 also allowed for taller buildings. In 1885, the first steel-frame skyscraper was built in Chicago. In 1913, the 60-story Woolworth Building was added to New York City's skyline. Methods of transportation changed, too. People in cities no longer traveled only by walking or riding horse-drawn wagons. They could take electric streetcars instead!

FIRST LIGHT BULB

Many things produced during the Industrial Revolution are still used today, such as the electric light bulb.

WOOLWORTH BUILDING

SHAPING AMERICA'S CITIES

The Industrial Revolution brought quick change to America's cities. Despite the hardships caused by cities' rapid growth, there were also many improvements. When labor laws were created or changed, immigrant and migrant workers' lives changed for the better. Advances in technology helped make life easier for many people. Roads, railroads, streetcars, sewer systems, and garbage collection systems were created. We still use these things today.

As working and housing conditions improved, an increasing number of people of similar social and economic backgrounds were able to move to the same neighborhoods. Many of these neighborhoods are still well-known, such as New York's Little Italy and San Francisco's Chinatown. The efforts of America's immigrants and migrating people helped shape its most important cities.

GLOSSARY

custom: A traditional way of life of a group of people.

decade: A period of 10 years.

immigrant: A person who comes to live permanently in a new country.

industrialization: The process of developing industries on a large scale.

material: The matter from which something is made.

migrate: To move from one area to settle in another.

rebel: To go against authorities or established ways of doing things.

reformer: A person who makes changes to something in order to make it better.

reputation: A belief generally held about someone or something.

sewer system: An underground network of pipes that carries water and waste away from homes and businesses.

technology: The way people do something using tools and the tools that they use.

tenement: During the Industrial Revolution, a building that housed many families. It was usually rundown, in bad condition, and occupied by the poor.

textile: Having to do with cloth.

union: An organized association of workers formed to protect and further their rights and interests.

INDEX

PRIMARY SOURCE LIST

Page 9 (inset). New York City tenement house with children in front. Created by Lewis Wickes Hine. Photograph. February 1910. Now kept at the Library of Congress Prints and Photographs Division, Washington, D.C.

Page 13. Boy working in basket factory. Created by Lewis Wickes Hine. Photograph. October 1908. Now kept at the Library of Congress Prints and Photographs Division, Washington, D.C.

Pages 14–15. Joseph J. Ettor speaking at an IWW demonstration. Created by the Bain News Service. Photograph. May 1913. Now kept at the Library of Congress Prints and Photographs Division, Washington, D.C.

WEBSITES

Due to the changing nature of Internet links, PowerKids Press has developed an online list of websites related to the subject of this book. This site is updated regularly. Please use this link to access the list: www.powerkidslinks.com/soim/city